Looking for Pets

Written by
Stephen Rickard

Illustrated by
Heike Jane Zimmermann

I am going to go for a run with my pet dog, Rex.

I am looking for my dog, but I cannot see him.

Rex is not in my garden and he is not in my bedroom.

Will you look for my dog with me?

Yasha has a pet cat, Moon. Moon needs to go to the vet for a check-up.

Yasha is looking for her cat, but she cannot see her.

Moon is not in her bed and she is not on her rug.

Vikram and Jameela will look for Moon with Yasha.

Will you look for Moon with them?

They are all looking for Moon.

They all look in the bedroom.

They all look under the bed.

They all look under the chair.

They cannot see Moon.

"Look! I can see Moon," Vikram tells Yasha. "She is in the garden."

They all go into the garden.

Moon is sitting in the yard. She is sitting with Rex.

Now Rex can go for a run and Moon can go to the vet for her check-up.

Will you go with them?